PUBLISHED BY ROBERT

CORBIN

OVER THINKING

Published By Robert Corbin

@ Alan Scott

Over Thinking: Take Your Life to the Next Level

All Right RESERVED

ISBN 978-87-94477-98-7

STABLE OF CONTENTS

Chapter 1 1

Thinking With Optimism 1

Chapter 2 8

Why Positive Thinking Is Not Enough 8

Chapter 3 14

Understanding Barriers To Positive Thinking 14

Chapter 4 25

The Power Of Positive Thinking: An *Introduction* 25

Chapter 5 29

Positive Thinking Explained 29

Chapter 6 36

How To Not Take Things Personally? 36

Chapter 7 49

The Road To Positive Thinking 49

Chapter 8 59

Overcoming Stress 59

Chapter 9 73

How The Law Of Attraction Works With Your Beliefs.... 73

Chapter 10 79

Building Resilience Through Positive Thinking 79

Chapter 11 84

Beyond The Individual: Positive Thinking And Social
Change 84

Chapter 12 90

Knowing What You Want In Life 90

Chapter 13 98

The Subtle Art Of Self-Belief 98

Chapter 14 126

Ways To A Stress-Free Life 126

Chapter 15 135

Learning To Relax 135

Where To Find These Limiting Beliefs 139

Chapter 1

Thinking with optimism

HAVE MANY COMMITMENTS

Thinking no: "I have too many things to do, I feel like I'm going crazy and I don't even know where to start."

Thinking yes: "I have a lot of things to do, so I postpone the less urgent ones and delegate to others what I can avoid to shouldering."

TO BE VERY TIRED

Thinking no: "I'm wrecked, but I can't rest yet because I have to fix my house."

Thinking yes: "Now I'm really tired and I think I deserve some rest. I'll fix up the house later or tomorrow; certainly only if I feel like it."

WAIT FOR THE PAY RAISE

Thinking no: "I'm very upset because my boss still hasn't told me if he'll give me that pay raise I've been asking him for a long time."

Thought yes: " I think I deserve the pay raise I asked for a month ago. My boss has had plenty of time to think about whether it's right to give it to me, so today I can safely go to him and ask him what he has decided about it."

PRACTICAL RULES

To become more and more adept at turning any situation to one's advantage, it is necessary to always keep in mind the rules that follow and that form the basis of positive thinking.

BEING LATE

Thinking no: "My God, I'm late: I'm a real disaster, I can never win my fight against time."

Thinking yes: "I'm late, but I'll catch up. Because whoever wants to can!"

LITTLE SUGAR IN THE CAKE

Thought no: "I put a little sugar in the cake, so it'll taste less good than usual."

Thought yes: "I put a little sugar in the cake, so it will be less cloying and less caloric, all to the benefit of the diet.

IT'S A NICE DAY

Thought no: "It's sunny: I'm not going out because I have to do the laundry."

Thinking yes: "It's sunny: I go out and enjoy it."

TO RECEIVE AN INVITATION TO A PARTY

Thinking no: "I wish I didn't go to the party tonight, because I never know how to behave with people I don't know."

Thinking yes: "I can't wait to go to the party tonight because definitely, I will meet interesting people. I like to listen to other people talk and I'm sure other people like to listen to me."

JUDGING THE CLEANING LADY

Thought no: "The lady who helps me with my housework certainly scams me, so much so that she never dusts off the top shelves."

Thought yes: "The lady who helps me with the housework is pretty good, but she never dusts the top shelves. I think it's only fair to point that out to her."

LOOK FOR THE LIKE SIDE:

It is useful to constantly look for the most pleasant side of any circumstance, trivial or important, learning to ignore how much negative it can present. To give an example, when you happen to get stuck in traffic (a highly stressful situation), instead of huffing and puffing thinking about the time you are wasting, take advantage of it to relax listening to music, or to fantasize about something very pleasant or, again, to look around to discover how funny are the expressions of those who get so angry when they get stuck in cars. It will be extraordinary to realize that, in doing so, time passes much faster and that, all in all, it is not so terrible to spend a few minutes alone with yourself.

AVOID PHRASES AND NEGATIVE WORDS:

for example, you shouldn't say: "I'm not afraid of that interview," but it's better to say: "I'll face the interview calmly and quietly. That is, words that evoke discomfort (for example, the words fear, death, terror, anguish and so on) should be banned from your vocabulary.

3) SPEAK TO THE PRESENT AND NOT TO THE FUTURE:

For example, one should not say: "When I face that interview I will be calm," but rather it is better to say: "When I happen to have an interview I am calm."

NOT LET ONE'S GUARD DOWN:

there are circumstances in which it seems that you no longer have the strength to look for the best side of what you are experiencing or have to face. However, it is imperative not to lower one's guard, after winning the first battles, when faced with situations that are objectively not easy, positive thoughts begin to emerge automatically and the constructive mental attitude becomes part of one's personality.

START THE DAY BY MAKING A BEAUTIFUL SMILE FROM THE MIRROR:

smiling immediately makes you feel better, so it is worth turning the first smile of the day to yourself, looking in the mirror. Also, it's a good idea to say to yourself every morning: "Today will certainly be a good day, full of news and pleasant situations."

Chapter 2

Why Positive Thinking is Not Enough

If you think about those for a second though, what does, "Just do it" mean? Just do what? And, does it mean to, "just do it" instead of considering the ramifications of "it" first? Or, is it the opposite of the concept of, "Look before you leap?" On the other hand, is it saying to just do that thing instead of some other way of approaching it? The point is that the phrase is vague and intentionally so.

What about, "Think different"? Different than what? If you understand what this phrase means, how exactly do you go about thinking different? Is thinking different thinking the opposite of thinking like the norm? Is it thinking of different strategies, or is it changing the structure of your thinking itself? All of these questions are intentionally unanswered.

And yet, they are exciting phrases. The concept of just doing it makes you feel like a power center of action and thinking differently conjures the idea of thinking brilliantly outside the box. Yet, then again neither of these talk about **how** to do what they suggest.

"Just think positive," is a phrase similar to these two. It's inherently compelling but almost completely empty of useful direction. The phrase seems to exist in a world where it's possible to just not experience negativity at all. And you know that's not true. But even if it were, the phrase makes you inspired with no clear direction of what exactly to do.

That's because, "Just think positive," is not a prescription or a set of instructions. It's often said with good intention and it's possible for it to be exactly what you need to hear at the time you hear it. This is because language requires a person to make meaning from it, and everyone experiences language differently. So, it's possible that, "just think positive" can be helpful for a lot of people.

It can even form the basis for your philosophy of life complete with rosy-colored glasses and unshakable faith in the inherent goodness of all things. That kind of world view is wonderful.

But, if you've tried adopting that philosophy and found yourself wanting, then this book is for you.

The biggest most obvious gap in this way of living is the question: What do you do when thinking positive doesn't solve the problems of your life?

Let's say you have a friend you can't stand being around, but you don't have the heart to make the necessary changes to get space from them. Does,

"Just think positive" mean that you should ignore all of your feelings about them and try to look on the bright side? What usually happens from this kind of approach? You end up resenting them even more.

Let's say you've got bills coming in the mail and you don't have enough money to pay for them. What do you do? The phrase says to just think positive! So, you start chanting affirmations that you don't believe, because they don't reflect your reality. You try to ignore them but your debt and situation worsens. Finally, you blow up at a collections caller one day because you just can't take trying to have those nice thoughts anymore!

What if you've got a dream that you really want to create, but you have no idea how to do it? You keep hoping , but really you doubt that it will ever work for you. Instead, you paper over how you really feel with false optimism. Meanwhile, other people you know keep getting more and more of what they want. Finally, you just give up on that dream.

"What's their secret? I'm thinking positive dammit!"

It's not your fault.

And it's not the fault of someone who gave you the advice. Not everyone needs the same tool. This book is for people who've tried to think positive but found that they still can't get what they want. This book will show you that there are deeper things going on in your vibration. Your beliefs can be changed and you can eventually think positive in an organic, truthful way to yourself.

I've found that thinking positive isn't enough, but it doesn't mean it doesn't have merit. Optimism is a healthy thing, but if you have things that you've wanted in your life for a long time, you have limiting beliefs that simply thinking positively aren't going to dislodge.

Just thinking positively isn't a comprehensive enough answer to getting the things that you want. It's as reductive as saying, "just make money" to someone in a financial predicament or, "just get a date" for someone who is lonely and looking for love. Ironically, the people who are already getting what they want can just think positive a lot of the time, but that's because they are aligned to what they want already.

For the rest of us, there is a better way. But, we have to lay some groundwork first.

Chapter 3

Understanding Barriers to Positive Thinking

Negative Thought Patterns

Negative thinking patterns, often known as cognitive distortions, frequently prove to be formidable adversaries in the maze of human cognition. Finding the cryptic hints these obstacles leave behind is frequently the first step in the fight to get past them. They resemble persistent anti-optimism saboteurs; they linger in the shadows of our minds, waiting for an opening to disrupt our mental peace.

Catastrophizing (imagining the worst-case scenario), black-and-white thinking (perceiving things as either good or terrible, with no gray regions), and overgeneralizing are examples of negative thought patterns (basing broad conclusions on single events). Positive thinking is obstructed by these tendencies because they drain positive energy and replace it with self-doubt and fear.

Self-Limiting Beliefs

The mental chains that bind us to the boundaries of our comfort zones are self-limiting ideas. They are the reverberations of a sneaky self-narrative that persuades us that we are unable to accomplish particular objectives or results. These ideas essentially lead to a self-fulfilling prophesy because we rarely aim for things we've previously determined are unreachable.

These self-limiting ideas typically have their roots in previous setbacks, rejections, or painful experiences. We connect these instances to our identities rather than seeing them as isolated incidents, which feeds the belief that we are essentially flawed or destined for failure. This false impression creates a cloudy lens through which we view our abilities and self, which inhibits our ability to grow personally and cultivate a positive outlook.

External Influences on Thinking

People are inherently influenced by the attitudes, behaviors, and views of others since they are social beings. While these outside forces can act as catalysts for good change, they can also have negative impacts, especially when they encourage pessimism.

Our mental toughness can be weakened by social expectations, unhealthy relationships, social media's constant inspection, and the constant barrage of bad news. We may develop a type of mental myopia as a result of this constant barrage of negativity, losing sight of the good in the midst of the bad. To keep a strong and healthy mindset, it is essential to cultivate mental resilience and to carefully choose our external influences.

The Road to Positive Thinking

Life-changing events can occur at any time, and everything happens for a purpose. They can either lift you up or knock you down, but ultimately, it is up to you. All of it is in your head. The same thing happens to you, your neighbor, your coworkers, and your friends; what distinguishes you from them is how you choose to accept, respond to, and perceive the situation.

Each and every human experience has two sides, exactly like a coin. It has both a positive and a bad aspect, but the positive aspect is more significant and has a different effect. Although you can only see one side of a coin when you flip it and hold it in your hand, this does not limit your options. You must turn things around to develop positive thinking skills. There is another side to everything.

There are two options available to you, for instance, if your employment application was unsuccessful. You might give up looking for work and depress yourself by labeling yourself a failure. You don't need to keep wishing that you will succeed in your career; simply stay put. You might also persuade yourself as you leave the interview that the position isn't appropriate for you and that you will find something better. After doing this, you continued your job search in the hopes of finding another position. The likelihood of success is automatically lost if you select option one. You are denying yourself the chance to experience happiness. For the second choice, the opposite is accurate. By selecting the second alternative, you commit to making progress in the direction of your objective.

When you have been suffering through a bad situation for a while, like a divorce or a "hopeless" job search, you have probably heard others say that there is light at the end of the tunnel. The cliche that says you need to have hope and that the bad things won't stay forever is true.

It takes a lot of faith to think that anything good may come from something bad. People often have a predisposition to be skeptical about seemingly miraculous events. Why would a terrible thing lead to a good thing? What you are going through is not actually bad, that's the problem. Everything that is negative is simply a creation of your thoughts. Once you allow yourself to think it is, it will only turn negative.

While it's also true that optimism cannot be learned overnight, it is something that may be learned with time and effort. You might have thought that being optimistic is merely a mental exercise. Well, it's partially true, but not fully. Being optimistic also involves your actions and words. It may be built with the words you select and the ideas you permit to enter your head.

Focus on Your Goal

Nothing you do will get you closer to your objective than concentrating on it, no matter what you do. To avoid being lost, keep your end goal front of mind at all times. Don't consider a job interview failure as losing your chance to achieve. You'll remain motivated as you work toward the objective if you keep it in mind. For instance, perhaps you need to find work so that you can support your family, buy a house, and drive the automobile of your dreams. What is driving you?

Focus provides you direction, and when you have a plan for getting there, you can still find your way back if you wander off course. Do you recall hearing that it's better to start late than never? Here, it essentially means the same thing. Being able to motivate yourself again by being able to remind yourself of why you are doing something has power in and of itself.

Gratitude

Thankfulness is quite powerful. Gratitude and happiness, in my opinion, go hand in hand. You're considerably more likely to produce happiness in your life when you're grateful for the abilities or possessions you have. For instance, you might be thankful for the chat you had yesterday with a friend or family member or for your ability to successfully communicate with your coworkers by outlining how important your ideas are to the accomplishment of a specific project. Even showing gratitude for basic necessities like food to eat, the ability to walk, or being loved can make you feel happier and more joyful.

Getting what you want when you want it is not always a guarantee of happiness. It frequently entails contentment and gratitude for what you already have. You might be wondering how on earth you can understand anything like failing a job interview after reading this. It just indicates that you were not the person they were searching for and that there is something better out there for you. It does not imply that you are a failure.

The more interviews you have, the more comfortable and competent you will become. Perhaps you learnt something from the conversation or from your experience that you can be thankful for or appreciative of, allowing yourself to grow for your next interview and learn from your mistakes.

Condition Yourself

A machine needs conditioning in order to run efficiently. Your body need a warm-up every morning in order to operate at its best. This idea applies equally to how you spend your life. A ritual or practice can significantly improve this situation. What actions can you take to train yourself to feel joyful every day?

A few suggestions are doing 50 jumping jacks to get your blood pumping and feel rejuvenated, being thankful for your life and the ability to breathe, or repeating positive affirmations to yourself to remind yourself of all the wonderful attributes you possess.

Be Persistent and Resilient

Life is an adventure. You will fall behind if you don't keep moving forward. Always challenge yourself to try out new things and keep going forward, even when things are difficult. There can be barriers in your path, but you can always remove them. You have a creative and resourceful mind by nature. They are obstacles, but you can work around them and get through them.

Don't Just React; Respond

A reaction is a prompt response to a circumstance. When you come upon anything, it acts like an automatic reflex. You instinctively pull your hands away from a hot stove when you touch it by accident. Despite the fact that this reaction is the body's natural defense system, it cannot handle all situations. Sometimes, in order to defend yourself, you must act first and then ponder, or respond rather than react.

You instinctively go for any meal you see when you're hungry. When you react, you consider quick and easy ways to get food as well as future hunger prevention strategies. Being reactive to the situation is insufficient if you want to be an optimistic person. Do not simply cry, give up, or stop moving. Every setback should be followed with planning how you can overcome the same challenges in the future. That is how we develop personally.

Chapter 4

The Power of Positive Thinking: An *Introduction*

The Science Behind Positive Thinking: Research in psychology and neuroscience has shed light on the science behind positive thinking. It has shown that our thoughts and emotions can shape our brain's neural pathways, leading to changes in our perception, behavior, and even physical health. The brain's plasticity allows us to rewire our thought patterns and develop a more positive outlook on life.

Benefits of Positive Thinking: Positive thinking offers a multitude of benefits that extend to various aspects of our lives. Studies have shown that it can improve mental health by reducing stress, anxiety, and depression. It enhances our resilience, enabling us to bounce back from challenges with greater ease. Positive thinkers tend to have stronger immune systems, better coping skills, and higher overall life satisfaction.

Shifting Mindsets: Cultivating a positive mindset requires intentional effort and practice. This chapter explores various techniques and strategies to shift our mindsets from negative to positive. We delve into topics such as reframing negative thoughts, practicing self-compassion, embracing gratitude, and adopting an abundance mindset. By incorporating these practices into our daily lives, we can rewire our brains and experience the transformative power of positive thinking.

Overcoming Barriers to Positive Thinking: While positive thinking is immensely beneficial, it is not immune to challenges. This chapter examines common barriers that hinder our ability to embrace positive thinking, such as self-doubt, fear of failure, and negative influences in our environment. It offers practical tips and insights on how to overcome these barriers and develop a resilient and optimistic mindset.

Creating a Positive Thinking Routine: Building a positive thinking routine is crucial for long-term success. This chapter provides guidance on incorporating positive thinking practices into our daily lives. It explores techniques such as positive affirmations, visualization, mindfulness, and the power of self-talk. By integrating these practices into our routines, we can reinforce positive thinking and make it a natural part of our mindset.

Conclusion: Chapter 1 has laid the foundation for understanding the power of positive thinking. It has explored the science behind it, highlighted its numerous benefits, and provided practical strategies for cultivating a positive mindset. As we continue through this book, we will delve deeper into specific areas where positive thinking can make a significant impact, such as relationships, health, and personal growth. By embracing the power of positive thinking, we can unlock our full potential and create a life filled with joy, resilience, and fulfillment.

CHAPTER 5

POSITIVE THINKING EXPLAINED

To live a happy and progressive life all individuals need to be positive thinkers. Positive thinking is a mental attitude in which you expect great and favorable results. In other words, positive thinking is the process of creating thoughts that make and transform energy into reality. People who exercise positive thinking are those who always anticipate success, health, and happiness. They know that no matter how difficult situations are in the present or have been in the past, there will always be light at the end of the tunnel. Positive thinking is known to be effective in changing lives because it influences how you feel and the actions you take. It is meant to put you on the right track and ensures you to put efforts into making great achievements. Obviously, nothing comes easy in life, but with the right mindset, it becomes a smooth sailing journey. All one is left with is aligning the goals they have in mind with their actions.

I won't forget to mention that there is so much power in positive thinking and applying it your life along other survival skills could do you so much good. I say this because there are so many people who don't give the idea of positive thinking much credit. It has actually gained so much popularity and to effectively use it, one needs more than just the awareness of its existence but rather adopt it in all that you do. I encourage you to be a positive thinker as a way of developing a positive attitude which ultimately attracts happy and pleasant feelings. All this is necessary to our health and general wellbeing. It could be difficult to maintain positive thoughts in life due to the difficulties and challenges we experience in our day to day lives, but once you understand its worth, then you will try much to achieve it. You have nothing to lose by being more positive because negative thinking adds absolutely no value to your life.

When you think about positive thinking, it is much about your outlook on life and how you approach different things like failures, loss, etc. This kind of mindset makes it easy for you to deal with them. Positive thinking doesn't, however, mean that you bury your head in the sand and forget about all of the life's experiences and situations that are not pleasant. It is all about approaching the negative in a more productive and healthy way that ensures your general wellbeing.

It may not directly give you all you want in life, but positive thinking will create real value in your life and allow you to cultivate skills that last long. I can't say the same about negative thoughts because all they do is narrow your thinking and it makes you focus your everything on the dark side of life and could result in stress, lack of energy, lack of self-esteem, etc. In this state you tend to ignore all relevant opportunities to create solutions and progress. Generally, the worst thing about negative thoughts is that they drain you of all your energy and prevent you from living in the present. You will never notice how deep you are drowning because the more you give in to your negative thoughts the stronger they become and they will be in control of a big part of your life than you could realize.

THE MAIN BENEFITS OF POSITIVE THINKING

If there are benefits you could easily enjoy, then they are those of positive thinking, which unlike any other thing in life, they are always felt immediately. It might not be all you need in life but it is most of it. Positive thinking is believed to have a significant effect in all areas of a person's life, and its most basic is that it creates real happiness. Personally, I would give anything to be happy as it has proved to be something of real worth. Many of us are searching for other things like wealth in life, forgetting that to enjoy them fully they need to be built on the foundation of happiness. It is necessary that you get to learn about the benefits of positive thinking because it will give you more than a reason to exercise it. It gives you an idea of how your life transforms if you learn to apply it in your daily life. Explained below are the benefits of positive thinking:

Resilience:

Instead of you falling apart in the face of challenges and difficulties, positive thinking makes you more resilient. This is so because it will focus all your energy on the positive side of things, saving you from too much worry or sadness. The resilience will be noticed in your ability to move on with life and also overcome all kinds of obstacles.

Improves your health:

We all know that health conditions like stress, anxiety, and depression are as a result of negative thinking. By being a positive thinker then you reduce the risk of such conditions, and you will lead a healthier and happier life. When your mind and heart are troubled, then the chances are that your body won't function normally. Thinking positively should not be an option but rather a necessity if you want to lead a healthy life.

Overcome fear:

Fear can be very crippling, both mentally and emotionally as it takes over us completely. With positive thinking, an individual can conquer any kind of fear as your mind will only think of the good that should come your way.

Improves relationships:

A person who has positive thoughts always creates positive atmospheres and feelings. It is an essential tool in building healthy relationships as it makes you relate better with people and thus creates room for improved relationships.

Builds real happiness:

Another fact about thinking positively is that it makes you and the people around you happy. Hence, you will always be at peace and you will have the ability to influence the way others think and feel.

Increased confidence:

With positive thoughts you tend to be very comfortable in your own skin and you will appreciate your life fully. You will have the heart to face all that comes your way, as a result, you are a more confident and brave person.

CHAPTER 6

HOW TO NOT TAKE THINGS PERSONALLY?

There is only one way to avoid criticism: do nothing, say nothing, and be nothing. If you do anything, people will have something to say about it. With the freedom of speech comes the freedom to criticize. Amazingly, everyone has an opinion on how you should live your life.

But criticism is an essential part of life. It shows you are doing something. Criticism is the price you pay for having ambition. If you never face criticism, you may not be doing much that makes a difference. Learning not to take criticism personally is something we all can benefit from. Take criticism seriously, but never personally. If it is valid, learn from it. Otherwise, just let it go. In this chapter, we will look at exactly how to do that.

It's not about you

Here's the truth - 99% of the time, how people behave is not about you. It's about them. Their behavior depends on a long list of underlying reasons. And even if you are on that list, you probably rank at the very bottom. There are several reasons that determine other people's behavior, and most of the time, they are not related to you at all. When someone disrespects you, be wary of the impulse to win their approval. Their disrespect is not a valuation of your worth. It is a signal of their character.

I cannot stress enough how important this is for your social interactions. If you do not internalize that people's behavior has nothing to do with you, you can never be truly free as far as your social life is concerned. Often people don't realize the price you paid to get to where you are today. They don't. And if you let each and every little comment shake you up, it's not healthy for your emotional health & self-confidence.

Let's look at an example. If a cashier in your bank acts rudely, you feel bad. That's pretty normal. You are a human being, and it is perfectly all right to feel bad if somebody misbehaves with you. BUT when you go home RAGING and think about that incident for hours… THAT is not normal.

It's a cue that you need to learn about not taking things personally.

People have many underlying issues and agendas

By going with the cashier example above, you repeat that incident in your head again & again, each time, feeling increasingly worse. Along with your hatred towards that person, you might start to think about the REASONS for which he behaved in that way.

Now comes the crucial part... Because you do not have any more information about him, you put the entire blame on yourself. And these thoughts have a vicious cycle. Thoughts, generally, start from "maybe I said something bad" to "I always say something bad" to "I am not a good person" to "I deserved it!"

These thoughts are harmful to you. They hurt you on various levels – Your self-confidence, self-worth, emotional health, physical health, and your happiness.

Stop letting people who do so little for you control so much of your mind, feelings, and emotions. Remind yourself time and time again that other people have many underlying problems that are not apparent on the surface. If you could see what they are going through in their life, your hatred would turn into sympathy.

Maybe that cashier is having chronic back pain, making him irritating & rude, or perhaps he had a divorce yesterday afternoon, and his family life is in ruins. There could be a million reasons for his behavior that are not related to you at all.

Nothing others do is because of you. What they say or do is a reflection of their own reality, their own life. It says nothing about you but a LOT about them.

How can you be sure of what is going on in other people's head at any point in time? People will love you. People will hate you. And most of the time, it will have nothing to do with you.

They really don't know you personally, so you don't take what they say personally.

Different realities

Objective reality is an illusion. People live in their own little world and only see what they want to see. You will be shocked to find the number of times people are focused on themselves. You might think people are looking at you and judging your every move, but in reality, people are caught up in their own little bubble. Everybody is looking at the world from a different set of eyes.

A quote I love related to this topic (forgot who said it) – "when you are in your twenties, you think that everyone is thinking about you. When you are in your forties, you think that nobody is thinking about you. And when you reach your sixties, you realize that nobody was thinking about you at all."

It's a bummer that this kind of realization comes at a very late point in life. But that's where good self-help books & autobiographies can be so helpful. A person - who went through various hardships all his life - decides to put down all that knowledge in an easy to read book... That's called a real opportunity. You can learn what he learned and use it whenever you face a similar situation.

Reality is different for each one of us. And the biggest problem for all of us is the image in our heads of how life should be. Some people view the world as a nice place with endless opportunities. Others view it as a horrible place where everybody else is out to get them. What we see with our eyes does not get straight into our minds untouched. It gets through many 'filters' first.

What we see gets filtered through our beliefs, our worldviews, memories of our past experiences, our attitude, our physical state, and even our current mood. These filters COLOR what we see and hear.

Let's say somebody plucks a flower from a tree; what would you think? Would you get angry thinking what will happen if all people start doing that? Soon, there will be no flowers left in that tree. OR would you feel happy thinking that people do take time to admire little things in life, even in this fast-moving world...?

Notice the difference?

The meaning of an event is whatever you ascribe it to be. Objective reality only exists in our minds and nowhere else.

Don't let other people's opinion of you become your reality. They have a different view of the world, its people, and how things are. Don't blame yourself. It's not about you. You can try everything in your power to change their perception, and you will fail.

It took years of life experience to get an individual's perception up to this point. You cannot change it in an instant. Don't even try. Instead, realize the truth that the final proof of greatness is to endure criticism without resentment. Let it roll right off you.

Good or bad, depends on you

No one is good or bad. It all depends on the situation and each person's perspective towards him or her. Whatever you believe will seem to be true. You cannot control other people & their outlook. You can only control yourself. I suggest you deliberately try to find the good in everything.

Why?

Because life is just too short to live in misery and blame everything. Life goes faster than you think. Ask anyone in his fifties or sixties about how fast they felt decades went by. The answer is always the same – "pretty fast!" So love, laugh, and try new things. Time will pass away. You can either spend it creating the life you want or spend it living the life you don't want. The choice is yours.

Never blame, complain, and take things personally. It's a fool's errand. Instead, focus on the more important things in your life, things which you are grateful for. Enjoy the little things in life because one day you will look back and realize they were the big things.

If somebody makes a sly comment on you or behaves rudely, brush it off. It's not about you. Think BIG and don't listen to people who tell you that it is impossible. Life is too short to think small. When someone tells you it can't be done, it's more a reflection of their limitation, not yours.

It is always better to forget and move on. Not everyone will understand your journey. That's ok. You are here to live your life, not to make everyone understand. It's no use trying.

How to deal with a persistent problem?

Sometimes, you will find yourself in a situation where it is not possible to forget and move on. What if one of your coworkers is rude or you have a family member who is always making negative comments. You will have contact with these people on a daily basis.

How to handle such a situation?

First, in the light of the above information, ask yourself – what else could this (behavior) mean?

This question will shift your focus to other possible meanings for an apparent bad behavior.

You will start to see reasons for their behavior that have nothing to do with you.

Second, if the person is constantly demeaning you, SPEAK UP. Let them know how you feel. A lot of times, people have no idea about how they are making you feel. Be clear. If there is a problem between you two, discuss and resolve it. Almost always, they will change their behavior around you.

If they don't, as the last straw, either minimize your interactions with that person or cut them out of your life completely. We already have enough problems. We certainly don't need more. Move to a new place. Shift to a different department. Get a new job. Do whatever you need to separate yourself from a situation like this.

As a side note, I would also suggest you work on building your self-esteem. Negativity does not affect a high self-esteem person emotionally. People with high self-esteem know their own values and don't identify themselves with other people's comments. They have control over their emotions and know how to deal with people effectively.

So that's it.

Knowledge has no value unless you USE it. Try to implement this information in your life. Even if it takes time, do it. It's worth it. Your happiness is worth it. Life is to be enjoyed, not endured. When you try to control everything, you enjoy nothing. Sometimes, you just need to relax, let go, and live in the moment.

Chapter 7

The Road to Positive Thinking

Everything happens for a reason and many things can change your life. They can knock you down or they can lift you up, but at the end of the day, it all depends on you. It's all in your mind. You, your neighbor, your workmates and your friends all experience the same thing but what makes it different is how you accept, react to, and view the circumstance.

Every human experience has two dimensions, just like a coin with two sides. It has both a negative component and a positive one, and one weighs heavier than the other, each one bearing different results. When you flip a coin and hold it in your hand, you only see one side, but it doesn't mean that you only have one option. There is another side that exists, and it is up to you to flip it around to train yourself to become a positive thinker.

For example, if you did not get accepted during your job interview, there are two things that you can do. You can give up the job hunt and tell yourself that you are a failure. You can stop hoping that you will be successful in your career and you can stay right where you are. Or you can exit the interview room, hold your head high and tell yourself that the job isn't right for you; you will get something better. With this, you went on to look for another job hoping that you succeed in your endeavor. If you choose the first, you automatically lose the chance for success. It is depriving yourself of the opportunity to be happy. The opposite is true for the second option.

Choosing the second option means taking steps to bring you closer toward your goal.

When you have been going through something negative for a long period of time, such as a divorce or "hopeless" job hunt, you've surely heard people telling you that there is a light at the end of the tunnel. This cliché statement is true in that the bad will not last forever, and that you need to have hope.

Believing that a positive thing would come out of something negative is not easy. It may sound miraculous event and people have the tendency to be skeptic about it. How can a bad thing yield a good thing? The thing is what you are going through is not really negative. The negativity of it all is just a product of your mind. It will only become negative once you let yourself believe that it is.

Though it is also true that optimism is not just something that can be achieved overnight, it is something that you can achieve with time and practice. You may have been thinking that optimism is just a matter of the mind. Well, there's some truth to it but not entirely. Optimism is also something that you do and say. It can be developed with the words you choose to use, and the thoughts you choose to let enter your mind.

Focus on your goal

In everything that you do, nothing will make you closer to your goal than focusing on it. Always keep your goal in mind so you don't lose your way. When you fail the job interview, don't think of it as losing your chance to succeed. Keeping the goal in mind will help you stay motivated as you work for it. For example, maybe you need to get job to support yourself, your family, buy a house, get that car you've dreamed about for years, etc. What is your motivation?

Focus gives you direction and when you know where you are going, even if you get lost along the way, you will still get back on track. Remember how people tell you that it's better late than never? It practically means the same thing here. The ability to remind yourself of why you are doing something has power in itself and can reenergize you.

Gratitude

Gratitude goes a long way. I believe gratitude and happiness are closely tied together. When your grateful for things or qualities you possess you're much more likely to create happiness in your life. For example, you might be grateful for the conversation you had yesterday with a friend or relative; or you might be grateful for your ability to communicate effectively with your co-workers, explaining how your ideas are imperative to the success of a particular project. Even being grateful for the things people take for granted, such as food to eat or the ability to walk or being loved, can bring in a refreshing sense of joy and happiness.

Happiness is not always getting what you want when you want it. Often times, it means being content and appreciating what you have. This might get you asking how in the world you can appreciate something like failing a job interview. It does not mean you're a failure, it simply means that you were not the person they were looking for and that there is something better out there for you.

Maybe you can think of the interview as practice and with each interview you have, the more confident and better you will get; maybe you learned something from the interaction or from your experience that you can be appreciative of or grateful for, allowing yourself to improve for your next interview you and learn from your mistakes.

Condition yourself

For a machine to function properly it needs conditioning. Your body, in order to optimally function, needs a warm-up every morning. This principle equally holds true in the way you live your life. That is where a ritual or routine can make a world of difference. What are a few things you can do to condition yourself to being happy every morning?

A few examples might include: 50 jumping jacks to get your blood flowing and feeling energized; or being grateful for being alive and breathing; or positive affirmations to remind yourself of the amazing qualities you have.

Be Persistent and Resilient

Life is a journey. If you don't keep moving, you'll get left behind. Always push yourself to try out new things and challenge yourself to keep moving forward even when the times get tough. There may be obstacles along the way, but you can always knock them down. You are naturally creative and resourceful. You will find your way around them and you have the ability to overcome them.

Don't just react; respond

Reaction is an immediate response to a situation. It is like a reflex that is automatic when you encounter something. When you accidentally touch a hot stove, you reflexively remove your hands from it. Though this reflex is a natural protective mechanism of the body, not everything can be managed with this simple reflex. Sometimes, to be able to protect yourself, you must think first before acting, or respond instead of react.

When you are hungry, you react by grabbing any food that you see. When you respond, you think of ways to get food in the shortest time possible and ways to avoid being hungry in the future. If you want to be an optimistic person, it is not enough that you just react to the situation. Don't just cry or give up or stop moving. Respond to every failure by thinking of ways that you can succeed the next time you encounter the same adversity. That is how we grow as individuals.

Chapter 8

Overcoming Stress

He is the great enemy of good living and the firstborn son of our troubled age.

But what is stress really? Contrary to the clichés, it does not necessarily represent the direct consequence of overly frenetic rhythms, super work, urgent commitments, and endless races against time.

Stress is, in fact, the body's response to external stimuli that frighten, disappoint, distress and, in general, are experienced by the mind as negative. Dissatisfaction, boredom, lack of goals, absence of satisfying stimuli, inability to give vent to one's anger and frustration are at the basis of the fearful accumulation of stress, responsible for a long series of disorders.

Among these disorders, the most frequent and severe are anxiety crises, invincible fatigue, changes in the heartbeat, and depression.

In order to fully understand that stress is a direct consequence of the inability to have a good quality of life, it is enough to think that various studies have shown that during a holiday period spent in boredom you can accumulate more tension than during a week of hectic work, from which, however, you derive great satisfaction.

The secret to overcoming stress is therefore, once again, to be positive about life, taking care to do everything in your power to gain advantage and gratification from any circumstance.

Let's see what are the rules that avoid the danger of getting caught in the insidious and harmful networks of stress, bearing in mind that they are an integral part of the beneficial philosophy of living well.

PRACTICAL RULES

LEARN WISHING WISH:

You must constantly try to understand what gives you pleasure and do what you can to get it. To love oneself means to protect oneself and the best strategy to implement this indispensable protection is to not stop thinking positively for a moment and to live in optimism.

SIMPLIFY TO MAXIMUM LIFE:

Establish some priorities and eliminate without regret all the useless commitments, which are perhaps fulfilled following habit. Besides, it is worth devoting some time to the elaboration of strategies that will make it possible to obtain, in all circumstances and in the face of any obligation, the maximum yield with the minimum effort. To give an example, why insist on washing your sneakers by hand (taking time out of something more pleasant) when you know very well that you can achieve the same, if not better, result by putting them in the washing machine?

CULTIVATE INTERESTS THAT MAY FUN:

Leisure activities must under no circumstances be transformed into other sources of stress. It is an excellent idea to get into the habit of meeting up with friends to play (the game, in adulthood, is liberating and rechargeable just as it was when you were a child), just as it is a way of loving sports, going to the theatre regularly, attending a recreation club.

LEARN TO Say NO:

Say no to those who ask too much, say no when you don't want to do a certain thing. Say no, simply, without bothering to look for excuses and without saying, reluctantly, yes if the famous excuses are difficult to find. The extraordinary thing about saying no is that nothing irreparable happens.

FORBIDDEN TO THINK CONTINUOUSLY TO EVERYTHING THAT NEGATIVE MIGHT HAPPEN:

If you feel well, nowhere is it written that the situation should get worse, as many people think, perhaps in deference to a misunderstood form of superstition. Every day you meet people who can't enjoy the moments of happiness because they fear that life may present a very heavy bill in exchange for them. But life is not a supermarket where "paying" is a must after taking: very often, contrary to what pessimists argue all the time, happy situations give rise to even happier events.

LEARN TO ACCEPT THE INEVITABLE:

Accepting difficulties is fundamental both to not live constantly under stress and not to waste energy measuring oneself against insoluble problems. If you are born with an ugly nose, if you have been fired, if you have been the victim of an accident or theft, if you are hopelessly late for an important appointment there are only two possibilities: swear, curse, self-pity, lock yourself up or look ahead trying to make the most of the situation (for example, since I have an ugly nose I will do my best to look more likable, more charming, more elegant). It is necessary to forbid oneself to think about how much of a negative could arise from the disadvantageous circumstance, imposing oneself instead to think only and exclusively about how much of a positive could emerge from the circumstance (for example, a delay can provide the opportunity to offer dinner or to give a little gift "to be forgiven" and therefore can help to reach a greater intimacy with the interlocutor).

Giving importance to WHAT YOU DO:

Always try to get at least a little satisfaction from what you are doing: you have to convince yourself that every action, even the most modest, has its own meaning and produces a result. It is wrong instead to dedicate yourself to any activity driven only by the force of inertia, because in this way you end up devaluing yourself, not loving yourself as you should. Instead, it is good to always attach great importance to the tasks that are being performed, even if they are humble and little recognized by others. Because they really do have that importance.

CARRY OUR LIFE:

You should never lead your life under the influence of others: you will have fewer regrets and less resentment, that is, you will accumulate less stress. The bad habit of preferring one thing to another just to please those who have given advice in this regard can only have a negative impact on the quality of life and thus become a significant source of stress. It is therefore essential to be convinced that it is right and natural that everyone is responsible for his or her own choices, just as he or she is called to account for his or her actions.

NEVER WAIT FREE:

For example, by buying something futile that you have been wanting for a long time or that is particularly attractive. Money should be used to make life better: never forget it. Continuous renunciations are in fact inexhaustible sources of stress, which is worthwhile, as far as possible, to stem. So it is right and not "sinful" to begin to say yes, at least sometimes.

SINGING:

As soon as the opportunity arises, one must sing, overcoming inhibitions, regardless of whether one is or is not in tune. Singing is liberating, it releases discontent, it relieves tension, it gives new energy. Even better is being able to sing in a group, with friends, perhaps accompanied by the sound of a guitar. However, there is nothing to be ashamed of even singing alone, so much so that singing is a universal practice, widely used in most cultures as an instrument capable of producing satisfaction.

SOAK HANDS IN WATER:

When the tension is strong and you find yourself unable to resort to the relaxation technique (explained in the last chapter) it can help to place hands and wrists under fresh running water, taking care to wet your temples as well. The water helps to eliminate the accumulation of negative energy and has a revitalizing action that is worth taking advantage of.

SHOES:

Shoes are a strong constraint for the foot, which tends to affect both body and mind. You should also always choose comfortable and elegant clothes, in which you feel comfortable in all respects. It may seem strange, but inadequate clothing, uncomfortable or out of tune with one's personality, encourages the accumulation of stress and makes it more difficult to relieve tension.

CULTIVATE FANTASY:

Imagination is an extraordinary source of pleasure both because it cannot be harnessed by anyone and because it allows you to live satisfying situations which, even if they are the result of imagination, can be useful to relieve tension or, at least, to push away negative thoughts. Surrendering to fantasies that gratify is therefore one of the most effective ways to relax, as well as a way to live better and to train yourself to think positively. Fantasy can be used with excellent results both to make otherwise monotonous sexual intercourse appetizing and to pass the time pleasantly when boredom threatens us.

FEATURING THE EXPECTED:

It may seem like a play on words, but it is actually a strategy to defend against stress. Man is a habitual animal and, as such, reacts negatively to anything that subverts his established order. But the unexpected is always lurking: it can happen to miss a train, or to find yourself in the need to postpone a fixed appointment, so it is good not to get too attached to the usual rhythms, just to be able to cope with an unexpected situation without problems. Imposing at least once a week to do something decided at the last moment can be considered a kind of vaccine against stress, which, in addition, leads to always looking for something better, as well as new.

TO TAKE THE RIGHT PAUSES:

During any activity give yourself a clear stop from the first signs of tiredness, discomfort, restlessness. It is enough to get up to take a walk in the room (if you are sitting down), drink a coffee, eat a chocolate, make a phone call to a friend to break the accumulated tension and resume what you were doing with more vitality, optimism and energy. Restarting work after a regenerating break means obtaining more fruitful results.

WIRE TO SOME OBJECTS:

Don't be ashamed to store and collect objects that may look ridiculous or in bad taste to a stranger's eyes, such as dolls, snow globes, model cars, old coins. In fact, objects in some way related to childhood exert a strong evocative and, in some ways, magical power on those who possess them, capable of giving carefree moments identical to those you feel when you are a child. Returning, even if for a few moments, to childhood represents another strategy to remove tension.

SPEECHING ABOUT OUR OPEN PROBLEMS:

Looking for someone to vent to, screaming with anger, rage, contempt, are all behaviors generally disapproved of by society but liberating. Keeping everything inside, swallowing toads, if on the one hand it can help (it doesn't necessarily happen) to be judged "extremely well-behaved people," on the other hand it can put a strain on the psycho-emotional balance.

DO NOT HESITATE TO ASK FOR HELP AND SUPPORT TO HEALTHY PEOPLE:

Whenever you find yourself in a difficult situation is wrong to shoulder the psychological burden of negative circumstances. It is also important to follow the rule of entrusting as much as possible to others all the tasks that you do not need to face yourself. Sacrifice to the utmost does not pay off and, what is more, only produces the catastrophic result of increasing the accumulation of stress and thus worsening the quality of life.

Chapter 9

How The Law Of Attraction Works With Your Beliefs

How do you become aware of what you're vibrating?

You do this by coming to terms with how you really feel about something you want. In other words, you have to really admit how you feel about something, which is hard to do. And it's why just thinking positively is not only not enough, it's unhelpful when you really try to uncover how you feel.

"The universe doesn't hear what you say. It hears what you mean." – Abraham Hicks

The universe cannot be tricked. That's because the universe is not a person who interprets what you want. Instead, it's more like a machine that responds to exactly what you're vibrating. The universe already knows what you want. You simply have to line up with the frequency of that. It seems simple on paper, but...

Words won't change what you feel. Instead, words can only help you understand and shift how you feel. You can shift how you feel by being willing to do the inner work.

Your beliefs block your ability to attract what you want

So why aren't you getting what you want all the time?

Think of yourself like a magnet. In your natural state you attract everything that you want to you that makes you truly happy. Everything. But, by the time you come to the point where you're making decisions in your life, you've accumulated erroneous beliefs that stop you from attracting what you want as easily or enjoyably as you want.

A limiting belief boils down to, "I can't have X without Y." It literally creates a limitation on what you want. These beliefs are like dirt or corrosion on your magnet. If you don't address them, your attraction power significantly decreases. When that happens, it becomes much harder to bring the things you want into your life in a way that's easy and fun.

When you change these beliefs it's like clearing the dirt from your magnet. You start attracting what you want in your life (what matches your frequency) automatically. Instead of trying to make what you want happen in your life through action, you'll congruently attract things into your life just by doing what you feel inspired to do.

This is why you can't just think positive to change the circumstances of your life. If your beliefs are holding back your ability to project your vibration clearly, then no amount of forcing yourself to think positive is going to clear those beliefs. In fact, when you shift the beliefs that are blocking you the most, you'll start getting more of what you want in the most easy and fun ways for you.

When you learn about anything, you filter it through your limiting beliefs. If you learned about the law of attraction already, then you probably learned about it through some kind of filter. That means you may intellectually get it, but be unable to practice the pure vibration to get what you want.

When you understand this perspective about how LOA works, you'll start doing the right actions – those that clear your vibration and give you the most vibrational leverage. You'll focus for a time on inner work, the work of shifting your vibrations and beliefs, and you'll experience results in a more organic, enjoyable way. Not only that, but the machine of reality will make sense to you and you'll know exactly what to do every time you have a new desire.

You'll stop beating up on yourself for not trying hard enough or thinking you missed an opportunity. You'll realize the power that you truly have and how to tap into it. And you'll see that this is an ongoing journey, one where you're continually strengthening the power of your magnet by clearing the dirt off of it.

When positive thinking is good.

For all the shit I've been giving positive thinking in this book, it's actually a great thing to do. The problem occurs when you use it as a tool to fix the wrong issue. Positive thinking won't shift your vibration, unless your vibration is fairly clean already. It will work for you if you're already getting some level of consistent success in the area that you want and you want to simply create more ease and flow in that area. So, positive thinkers, keep doing what you're doing. But, do me a favor and investigate your limiting beliefs first.

It's much more powerful to be positive, than to think positive.

What's the difference? Thinking positive is a conscious action that you take in order to try to reach a higher vibration. There's nothing wrong with that. On the other hand, being positive is what happens when you clear the dirt off of your magnet. You already are a positive attracting force, capable of creating anything you want. That sounds like a crazy statement, because you don't know your own power yet.

Chapter 10

Building Resilience through Positive Thinking

Understanding Resilience and its Importance

The graceful dance of life waltzes us through a rainbow of emotions, from exhilarating highs to agonizing lows. In this dance, an unrelenting constant? Change. Resilience proves itself in navigating these shifting sands. Resilience is the innate ability to adapt to adversity, to face the most challenging circumstances, and to come out stronger.

This captivating quality is more like air in our daily life than an abstract idea. Consider resilience as the key to overcome obstacles. It gives us a mental toolkit to handle everything from tiny annoyances to major life events, enabling us to overcome obstacles and advance in the face of uncertainty.

Avoiding difficulties is not part of being resilient. Instead, it is navigating them and coming out the other side, tempered and refined by the experience. An individual who is resilient views each setback as a milestone on the road to personal improvement rather than simply surviving obstacles.

Cultivating Resilience with Positive Thinking

What we sow grows in the ever-prosperous garden of the imagination. Therefore, the quality seeds for this garden—seeds that cultivate resilience—come from positive thought. It goes beyond just being a catchphrase or having a momentary cheerful outlook. In essence, it's a dynamic mental approach that sees obstacles as solvable and focuses on solutions rather than the issue at hand.

Resilience can be nurtured by encouraging an optimistic outlook. Together, these two qualities strengthen one another and form a solid mental foundation. They develop mental flexibility, a potent capacity for recovery, and the capacity to transform challenging circumstances into learning opportunities. Thus, optimistic thinking serves as the framework for building resilience.

Imagine a perennial tree that endures all four seasons unharmed. A robust mind pulls strength from positive thought, flourishing despite the harsh winds of adversity, much like this tree draws power from the earth. So resilience ceases to be an oddity and starts to become an inevitable result of a hopeful outlook.

Strategies for Bouncing Back from Challenges

One can ask how to successfully apply resilience and positive thinking in life after learning about its synergy. Mindfulness, solution-focused thinking, and developing solid relationships are some useful tactics.

Awareness of our thoughts, feelings, and behaviors is fostered by mindfulness. Being present allows us to see negativity, isolate it before it spreads, and therefore prune our mental garden. By having greater awareness, we may create an atmosphere that encourages optimistic thinking.

Thinking with a focus on solutions urges us to stop concentrating on problems and start looking for answers. It encourages innovation and resiliency, encouraging us to see challenges not as roadblocks but as turns toward an even better route.

The foundation of resilience is strong relationships. Human connection creates a network of support and a pool of shared resources for when things get tough. By boosting positivity and lightening our loads, the act of sharing a problem, asking for guidance, or simply expressing sentiments helps to build resilience.

Resilience is the compass needed to navigate the perilous voyage of life. Resilience, which is rooted in optimism, is an art and a science that turns obstacles into stepping stones. By mastering this symbiosis, we have the ability to gracefully dance with life's shifting rhythms and leave a lasting imprint on history.

Chapter 11

Beyond the Individual: Positive Thinking and Social Change

Promoting Empathy and Compassion: Positive thinking fosters empathy and compassion, essential qualities for social change. This section discusses how positive thinking can cultivate a deeper understanding of others' experiences, promote empathy, and encourage acts of kindness and compassion. It explores practical strategies for developing empathy, such as active listening, perspective-taking, and practicing gratitude. Readers will learn how positive thinking can bridge divides and foster unity among diverse communities.

Inspiring Positive Action: Positive thinking is a catalyst for positive action. This section explores how positive thinking can inspire individuals to take collective action for social change. It discusses the importance of values alignment and the pursuit of justice and equality. It explores how positive thinking can motivate individuals to engage in activism, volunteerism, and advocacy, amplifying their impact on social issues. Readers will gain insights into the power of positive thinking as a driving force for positive social transformation.

Building Resilient Communities: Resilient communities are essential for sustainable social change. This section delves into how positive thinking can contribute to community resilience. It explores how positive thinking can foster a sense of collective empowerment, resourcefulness, and collaboration within communities facing challenges. It discusses the role of positive communication, problem-solving, and collective decision-making in building resilient communities that can navigate adversity and drive positive change.

Creating Inclusive Spaces: Positive thinking promotes inclusivity and celebrates diversity. This section explores how positive thinking can create inclusive spaces where individuals from different backgrounds and perspectives feel welcomed and valued. It discusses the importance of fostering a positive and inclusive culture within organizations, educational institutions, and communities. Readers will gain insights into how positive thinking can challenge biases, promote understanding, and create environments that empower and uplift marginalized voices.

Educating for Positive Change: Education is a powerful tool for social change, and positive thinking can be integrated into educational settings. This section explores how positive thinking can be incorporated into curricula and teaching practices to nurture a generation of empathetic, resilient, and socially conscious individuals. It discusses the role of positive education in fostering emotional intelligence, social skills, and values-based decision-making. Readers will gain ideas on how positive thinking can be infused into educational systems to empower students to become agents of positive change.

Collaborative Solutions: Positive thinking encourages collaborative problem-solving and innovation. This section explores how positive thinking can facilitate collective efforts to address societal challenges. It discusses the power of collaboration, partnerships, and collective impact models in driving positive change. Readers will gain insights into how positive thinking can create opportunities for cross-sector collaboration, interdisciplinary approaches, and sustainable solutions to complex social issues.

Sustainable Practices: Positive thinking extends to sustainable practices and environmental stewardship. This section explores how positive thinking can inspire individuals and communities to adopt environmentally-friendly behaviors and lifestyles. It discusses the connection between positive thinking and sustainability, emphasizing the importance of collective responsibility and conscious choices for a healthier planet. Readers will gain practical tips on how positive thinking can drive eco-conscious actions and contribute to a more sustainable future.

Conclusion: Chapter 10 has explored the profound impact of positive thinking on social change. It has shown how positive thinking can elevate collective consciousness, promote empathy and compassion, inspire positive action, foster resilient communities, create inclusive spaces, drive educational transformation, encourage collaborative solutions, and support sustainable practices. By harnessing the power of positive thinking beyond the individual level, we can collectively create a more just, compassionate, and harmonious society. In the final chapter, we will reflect on the key insights gained throughout the book and provide practical guidance for integrating positive thinking into everyday life for long-lasting transformation.

CHAPTER 12

KNOWING WHAT YOU WANT IN LIFE

The whole idea behind knowing what you want in life is so that you can find meaning and purpose. It is a chance to create awareness of who you are as a person and what you set out to achieve. If you find yourself living in circles and by that I mean working hard, but you never seem to get anywhere worthwhile, then it means you didn't take some time to determine what you want in life.

For anyone to achieve satisfaction in life, they have to focus on things that they believe complete them. You are only aware of these things if you determine the exact thing you want in life and the path you would like to follow to achieve them. This should be applicable in all areas of your life. It is impossible to work towards achieving something when you have no idea what it is you want to achieve. Finding direction is important and will make it easier for you to make your dreams a reality.

It is a challenge for many to determine what they want in life, but if you are really ambitious about making a difference then you need to work at it. Below are important ways that I believe will help you know what you want in life:

Family and friends:

These are the people whom you spend a big part of your life with and could help you know what you want in life. They will advise on the things that they know you always enjoy and what they believe would be best for you depending on how well they know you.

Knowledge and skills:

There are always those specific things that you are excellent at and are equipped with the required knowledge and skills to progress in life through them. This could be something you studied in school or is a talent you grew with. Going back to yourself, analyzing and searching, will help you know who you really want to be in life. This will be the beginning of a great life.

Goal setting:

Another great way of knowing what you want in life is through setting goals. Have your short term and long term goals written down and they are the ones that will give you a clear idea of what you want in life. Goals have, for a long time, been known to be a source of motivation and direction and are exactly what you need.

Know where your happiness:

As I said the most important thing everyone should be in search of is happiness. If you are aware of certain things that always make you happy, then you already have an answer to the question at hand. Take some time to reach deep into yourself and know the kind of things that always make you happy.

I create value in my own life

This reminds you of your responsibility to always make yourself better in all ways and focus your efforts on doing things that only add value to all areas of your life.

I have what it takes to be a success

The truth is that we all have so much potential within us to achieve greatness, but if you lack this awareness, then you won't go far in life. As a person, it really helps to remind yourself every day that you actually have what it takes, and you will never give up on your dreams.

I appreciate myself and where I am in life

It is through self-love and appreciation that individuals can attain real success and happiness in life. This, therefore, means that self-appreciation makes you view the world differently and will help you approach life with more confidence and bravery.

I am very hard working

Apart from positive thinking, hard work comes in as a major factor in achieving goals and dreams. It is therefore very essential to remind yourself every day how hard working you are, and you will end up being exactly that.

My life is changing for the better

This affirmation is meant to help you be the kind of person who embraces change and does not allow any challenges or obstacles deter them from growing. It is also helpful in giving you the realization that your life is changing and that you are doing good work on that.

AFFIRMATIONS FOR GROWTH AND DEVELOPMENT

Affirmations are short sentences that are always believed to have a huge effect on a person's life. They normally affect the conscious and subconscious mind and their words bring up mental images that have the ability to motivate, inspire and energize. If you make it a habit of always repeating specific affirmations, then the resultant images brought about will influence a person's habits, behaviors, and actions. To achieve personal growth, it really helps to have in mind some of the best affirmations that align with your goals and dreams.

The truth is that we are what we think we are and by using affirmations you will have the power to be in full control of all your thoughts. This way you can direct them to focus on the things that are good for your general wellbeing. You, however, need to know that you can't only rely on thoughts and must work on transforming those thoughts into words and ultimately into actions.

The best thing is that the moment you affirm your dreams and desires you will be empowered with a sense of reassurance that your words will become your reality. The thing is, when you think of all your desires - your thoughts will create your reality. Explained below are important affirmations for your personal development that I believe will be of so much help:

My failures are a learning experience

Affirming to this every day gives you a different approach towards failure and helps you know that failure does not mean you are not good enough. The most successful individuals are those who understand that it is through failure that we grow and also through failure that we achieve great things.

CHAPTER 13

THE SUBTLE ART OF SELF-BELIEF

What are beliefs?

A belief is your sense of certainty about something. That's all. If you are CERTAIN about what something means, you have a belief about it.

There are two kinds of beliefs: conscious and subconscious.

The beliefs which we can NOTICE in our mind are conscious beliefs. We are aware of them. If someone asks you to write them down on a piece of paper, you can easily do it. For example: I am a good cook. I can dance well. I am a good person.

On the other hand, some beliefs are buried deep below our awareness. We cannot articulate them, but we can "feel" their effect. Let's look at an example. Kamal, a friend of mine, was a naturally expressive guy when he was among his friends. But anytime he found himself surrounded by a few unknown faces (like at a party), he felt "fear."

Now, it's completely normal for people to have little social anxiety, but this was something else. His face would become red and his palms sweaty. He felt threatened and wanted to get out of the situation as fast as possible.

He started taking therapy sessions, and after one year, he discovered the cause of this fear. Actually, when he was a little boy, his family went to attend a large carnival. There were thousands of people at that carnival.

He accidentally got separated from his family and got lost in the crowd. As a little boy, it was a terrifying experience. He was getting pushed by oncoming waves of unknown people. Some were looking at him weirdly. Some people tried talking to him, which made him even more terrified.

He was later found by the security and taken back to his family. He was fine, but after this frightening experience with unknown people, his subconscious mind formed the belief that "strangers are dangerous."

And he had been carrying this belief deep within his mind ever since, and it really hampered his social life. At the age of 32, he could not articulate WHY he felt fear. He only knew that social situations scared him.

But, after therapy sessions, he was able to uncover the hidden subconscious belief and remove it from his mind. Later, in this chapter, you'll discover ways to find your own limiting subconscious beliefs and how to remove them from your mind.

For now, let's return to the current topic. We all have many conscious and subconscious beliefs about different things in life.

Even now, you have beliefs about who you are (as an individual), how other people are, and what you deserve out of life. This applies to all areas of life: relationships, money, business, health, body, mind, etc.

In each of these areas, you have different beliefs that govern how successful you'll be in that particular field. This is true not only for you but for everybody. We all are confined by our beliefs. Research shows the amount of success an individual can have, depends MASSIVELY on where he "believes" his limit to be.

Let's take an example of people who suddenly win the lottery. Maybe they won a million dollars, but somehow they spend all that money and return to the condition they were in before they won the lottery.

This is a powerful example of limiting belief in action. These people subconsciously believe they do not deserve to have a million dollars, so they always find a way to spend it and return to their old condition.

Beliefs create the actual fact.

Top experts and coaches of the world like Anthony Robbins & Brian Tracy get you to change your beliefs so that they help you succeed instead of blocking you.

Further, both conscious & subconscious beliefs can be of two types: positive beliefs and negative beliefs. The beliefs that help you to reach your goals are called positive, and the ones that block you from getting what you want are called negative (or limiting) beliefs.

We want to identify and eliminate negative beliefs that are stopping us from becoming the kind of person we want to be and install positive, empowering beliefs that move us towards our goals.

It is critical because our beliefs affect the level of ACTION we take. If you have negative beliefs, then your mind will come up with hundreds of reasons why you'll never succeed and why it's better to give up right now.

On the other hand, having positive beliefs will be like having an internal coach, pushing you to move forward, regardless of the challenges you face.

Beliefs also affect your motivation levels. Positive beliefs provide certainty that you WILL reach your objective. That gives a big boost to your motivation.

And, just like action, motivation is also HINDERED by the presence of negative beliefs. A negative belief makes you think all the effort you are applying will eventually go to waste because you'll never reach your goal anyway.

As you can tell, beliefs play a very important part in achieving our objective of becoming a person with a positive mindset. It is critical that we get our beliefs to help us instead of stopping us from changing.

How your current beliefs are formed?

The majority of beliefs are formed during childhood when the brain is learning the ins and out of the world. And because the environment is so random, a child's brain forms the beliefs according to the conditions he is in.

For example, if a child grows up in a society where there is a lack of money, her brain is likely to form a belief that money is scarce and is something that is very hard to come by. On the other hand, a child who grows up in an abundance of money forms beliefs that money is abundant and easy to come by.

The surprising thing is the randomness of all this. Your negative and positive beliefs could be formed based on the environment you are in. It is completely random.

But here is the good news, you can change your beliefs at ANY point. When I started out, I had to change many of my negative beliefs and replace them with positive ones. It made a huge difference in the amount of success I had and my overall experience of life.

If you change your beliefs first, changing the action is much easier. Let me share a personal experience. When I was in high school, my elder sister gave me a pair of sunglasses. They were very nice and looked good on me. But I didn't wear them to school because I believed I wasn't "cool enough" to wear them.

Just normal sunglasses.

We don't become what we want. We become what we believe.

Beliefs change how we look at the world. Your reality is a reflection of your beliefs. They act as lenses from which we look at the external world and create its meaning. In the presence of positive beliefs, your outlook will be more positive. You will be able to find something positive even from a seemingly bad situation.

And in turn, negative beliefs will make you focus more on the problems, obstacles, and reasons why you should not even attempt to do something about your situation.

If you pay attention, then you can easily find people around you who have positive beliefs. We all have at least a few people who have a positive outlook on the world. These people are optimistic and full of energy.

I highly recommend you stick close to these people as much as possible. Because beliefs, like emotions, are CONTAGIOUS. The more time you spend with these people, the more your outlook will change to be positive.

How are beliefs created?

Remember our earlier discussion that beliefs are something you are REALLY certain about? Well, to get that certainty, we require "evidence" that those beliefs are true. These pieces of evidence are called references.

An example of a reference could be your boss giving you props for completing a report on time. This recognition provides evidence for the belief, "I am competent at my work."

The more references you have, the stronger the belief would be. For example, if a beautiful girl has been getting praise for her beauty since childhood, she will have thousands & thousands of references proving that she is beautiful. Now the belief would be so strong that she doesn't need to even think about it. It is certain in her mind -- she IS beautiful.

Imagine your beliefs like a table-top, and references are the legs of the table. Without legs, the table cannot stand on its own. That's exactly how your beliefs work. References create and hold beliefs together.

If you remove the legs (or even weaken them), the table-top will fall. Similarly, collecting many pieces of counter-evidence for a belief will weaken it and eventually remove it from your mind.

This is a very powerful concept. It gives us insight into how our beliefs work and how they can be changed.

If you want more details on how references shape our beliefs, read the book Awaken the Giant Within by Anthony Robbins. It's one of my favorite books on the subject of NLP and beliefs.

We will now use what we have learned to create positive, empowering beliefs while removing negative beliefs from our minds.

Effective ways to change your beliefs

Collect references that reinforce your positive belief

One of the most powerful ways to weaken your limiting beliefs while simultaneously strengthening a positive belief is to DELIBERATELY collect references for it.

To do this, think about two or three positive beliefs that will benefit you the most. These are the beliefs that you believe will be most helpful to have in your present situation. Now, take a new diary and write these beliefs down on the first page.

This is your table-top or the beliefs you want to have. Now you need to collect references (real-life evidence) to support your selected beliefs.

I would like to share a powerful secret with you. Your subconscious mind (where the beliefs are stored) does not give a damn about reason or logic. It never debates whether something is RATIONAL or not.

If you provide enough references, it will believe ANYTHING! You have the potential to have any belief you want in your life.

Now, as you go about your day, keep an eye out for anything which could even REMOTELY support your selected beliefs. For example, if one of your selected beliefs is "I am becoming a millionaire," then references to support that belief from your daily life could be:

- As you go about your day, consciously try to look at things in a more positive light. Even the smallest of incidents where you had a positive thought counts as a reference of belief - "I CAN change myself to become a more positive person."
- A very important part is writing down these references on a piece of paper or even on your mobile phone notepad. You are creating a written list of "references." Do not underestimate the power of written words.

- I am always on time, just like a millionaire who is punctual. I am going to be one.
- I worked the best I could today, just like the millionaires do. I have what it takes to be a millionaire.
- I have a dream to be a millionaire, and I am working in that direction, just like self-made millionaires did. I am like them. I am going to be one.
- A more suitable example would be – selecting a belief that "I CAN change myself to become a more positive person."

When you go to sleep at night, take out your list of references you made during the day and look at it for a few minutes. Now you see REAL WORLD evidence of positive thoughts that came into your mind during the day. It MASSIVELY boosts your self-confidence and strengthens your belief "I CAN change myself to become a more positive person."

In order to change, your mind craves proof (references) that you can become that type of person. And nothing could be more effective than a list of "real world" references that you collected during the day.

This list could be limitless. It only requires creativity and a positive approach. Any small, trivial thing could be your reference. You could even change the meaning of something negative and view it as a reference for your empowering beliefs.

For example, you want to start your own business but are doing a 9-to-5 job to pay your bills. If you are feeling bad about the current situation, you can change its meaning from "this is such a horrible situation. I am stuck here." to "You know what? This horrible experience is the universe's way of forcing me to work harder towards my goal: to create my own business."

You can change the meaning of any situation and view it as a reference to strengthen your empowering beliefs. Many people do it subconsciously... but they do it to reinforce NEGATIVE beliefs such as "people are mean," "money is hard to come by," or "I am not capable."

You will do it consciously... for the positive ones. As you find (or create) references during the day, write them down immediately on your mobile, so you don't forget them. When you come home, WRITE THEM DOWN in your diary as "evidence for belief..."

Writing down your thoughts on paper works like magic. It penetrates deep into your mind. Your collected references will create a deep sense of certainty about your selected belief.

As you continue to collect references for your beliefs, within 4-5 days, you will start feeling different. The belief will begin to feel VERY REAL.

If you continue to gather references for your empowering beliefs (which you should), they will become so ingrained in your mind that nothing will ever shake them out. You'll have rock-solid beliefs for the whole life.

Affirmations

Affirmations are positive statements that you repeat again and again to fill your mind with absolute certainty. In our daily life, we are constantly bombarded with countless messages from media like TV, newspapers, and magazines that we are not enough. We'll never be as good as "them." We can't have that. Etc.

Do you remember the TV commercial with a young, handsome guy with six-pack abs surrounded by six girls, or a female model with a perfect figure walking down the red carpet, or a celebrity arriving at a hot party in his Lamborghini?

While being completely harmless on the surface, this kind of exposure creates self-doubt in normal men and women about themselves. It subtly creates a "standard" in the minds of people which they believe they could NEVER reach.

What this does is to lower our confidence in ourselves and our capabilities.

And we need to fight against it. We need to RECLAIM our confidence and self-esteem.

This is where affirmations can help greatly. Affirmations will act as a daily reminder of your capabilities and value as a person. It will be your daily "boost" of confidence. It will protect your confidence against all sorts of BS thrown at you.

Incredibly successful people like Oprah Winfrey, Will Smith, Jim Carrey, Arnold Schwarzenegger, and Lady Gaga swear by the effectiveness of affirmations.

Affirmations really do work, but you have to use them correctly. I have been doing affirmations for four years now, and I can honestly say they made a significant positive impact on my life.

How to do affirmations correctly?

Write down your doubts and insecurities on a piece of paper. Then, identify five of your BIGGEST doubts and insecurities which you believe are holding you back the most.

2) After you have identified five of your biggest doubts, write down their exact opposite positive statement. For example, if your doubts statement is "I don't deserve to be rich," then its opposite positive statement could be "I fully deserve to be rich."

Change all five of your doubts into their opposite positive statements. Write them down on paper.

Make sure all your affirmations are positive and in the present tense. Don't make affirmations for the future, like - I will succeed in the future, I will have a fit body, etc. Your mind puts these statements in the "maybe in future" category.

Your affirmations must be positive and in the present tense. Example: I am successful, I deserve to be rich, I have a fit body, I have abundance in my life. Got it? Positive and present tense.

3) Now, after you have converted your five negative beliefs into positive ones on paper, write

down another five Positive beliefs which you believe will help you the most. These five beliefs are the mindset which you would want to have. For example, I am a good learner. I can deal with any situation.

You now have ten affirmations that you would like to have as beliefs. Five positive ones converted from your negative beliefs. And another five which you think are great to have. It's time to install these ten beliefs in your mind. Stand in front of a mirror (preferably full length where you can see your whole body) and look DIRECTLY in your eyes.

Say your affirmations out loud. Make sure to say them with PASSION & EMOTION, like you really believe them. You can use your facial expressions and gestures to bring up the emotions while saying your statements. This is important.

For example, if your affirmation is - I am going to be a millionaire, say it like you REALLY mean it! Change your posture. Stand tall, chest forward like you are proud of yourself. Put both of your hands up and shout "YESSSSSSSSS!" in a triumphant voice. FEEL the emotion and passion in your voice. Now repeat your affirmation two more times.

Do whatever you can to bring emotion into your affirmations. Statements mixed with emotions have a deeply penetrating effect on our minds.

Anthony Robbins (success coach, author of "Unlimited Power" & "Awaken The Giant Within") and Dr. Joseph Murphy (author of the bestselling book 'the power of your subconscious mind) stress the importance of mixing emotion in your affirmations. Without it, you would be doing affirmations for years without any benefit.

Do your affirmations daily. It only takes about 5 minutes, and within 2-3 weeks, you will start noticing changes in your behavior. If you keep doing it, these positive statements will become a permanent part of your mind.

I personally used this technique to change my beliefs, and it has worked amazingly well. It only needs a commitment on your part. Don't think about whether it will work or not. Suspend your disbelief and do it for a period of time. When you start noticing the difference, you would never want to stop.

Visualization

Visualization is a fancy word for 'vivid imagination' or 'imagined in great detail.'

It's a very effective technique for changing your beliefs. Medical science has proven that the human mind cannot differentiate between something vividly imagined and real life.

In an experiment, researchers have placed scanners on an athlete's body and got him to imagine running on a track in as much detail as possible. Scanners revealed that during visualization, his muscles were activating in the same manner as when doing the actual physical activity of running on a track.

Since then, multiple researchers have verified the positive effect of visualization on the actual performance of an individual. Now, this fact is widely accepted in sports psychology, and trainers put a significant emphasis on regular mental practice along with physical ones.

Now, here comes the interesting part - we know how beliefs are created and reinforced by 'real-life evidence.'

By using visualization, you can provide your subconscious mind any piece of "evidence" you desire because it CANNOT tell the difference between real life and something imagined in detail.

You can vividly imagine a scenario, and your mind will accept it as true. It essentially means is that you can "manufacture" evidence that will reinforce positive beliefs in your mind.

This is a very powerful concept, and its possibilities are virtually unlimited. For example, suppose you have social anxiety. You feel nervous about going to a party and talking to people you don't know. If you visualize for 10-15 minutes that you're in a party full of strangers and are feeling relaxed & calm while socializing with them, your mind will soon accept it as truth, and your social anxiety would decrease by a good amount.

I personally used visualization to get rid of my fear of public speaking. In the past, I had some pretty bad experiences with public speaking. I used to stutter my words, lose my train of thought, wondering what people are thinking about me while standing on stage. It was pretty embarrassing.

But when I found out about visualization and how it works, I decided to give it a try. So, on the night before my big presentation, I closed my eyes and visualized giving a speech in a room full of people.

I felt the same anxiety as when I stand on stage in real life. It was pretty much the same feeling. But, I forced myself to deliver my speech as best as I could. As this was in my imagination, whenever I messed up, I stopped & repeat it again and try to do it correctly this time.

It took 15 visualization tries for me to lose almost all of my anxiety while delivering my speech.

The next day, when I actually got on stage, it felt quite familiar. As if I had done it before. I did feel 'some' anxiety, but it was quite manageable. My speech went quite well, and people came up to me afterward to tell me how clear I was with my message.

Since then, I became a firm believer in the power of visualization. I used visualization in many other areas, and it always helped.

Anthony Robbins, Brian Tracy, Jack Canfield, Donald Trump, Napoleon Hill, Zig Ziglar, Dale Carnegie, and countless other extremely successful people firmly stand by the power of visualization.

The best classic books like- Think and grow rich, See you at the top, Power of your subconscious mind, How to win friends and influence people, etc. - recommend visualization as a tool to reach your goals faster.

On a personal note, the best resource I have found on the topic of visualization is Dr. Maxwell Maltz's book, Psycho-cybernetics. It has helped millions of people change their life for the better. I highly recommend checking it out.

Visualization is a very powerful technique, but you have to do it correctly. Follow this simple, step by step method.

Chapter 14

Ways to a Stress-Free Life

No matter what you do, and no matter how you try to avoid it, stress will always be there, waiting around the corner for you to come and get it. In fact, you need it to function properly. For example, you are preparing for an exam or work presentation tomorrow and you are feeling some stress about it. To relieve some of the stress, what you do is you study and prepare for it. Though stress here is something that you don't see as positive, your response to it is. The next thing you know is that you did very well of the exam or presentation! Imagine if you are not worried about your exam. The most likely thing you'd do is you won't prepare for it. Sometimes, not feeling the stress is more dangerous because you don't perceive any harm and your body as a harmless situation.

Stress takes on different forms. It can be mild, which is something that you can easily overcome, or it could be something more severe, something that can exhaust you of your energy and resources. Mild stress, just like the example given above, is helpful because it keeps you prepared for what's going to happen. But if the stress is so severe that you don't know what to do anymore, then it becomes harmful.

When you feel that you can no longer perform well in your job, or when you can no longer think straight, or when you think that you are not anymore getting the results that you want to achieve, you are likely undergoing severe stress. At this point, it is not advisable to continue with what you are doing. Just like a machine that has been excessively used, people inefficiently function when they are under severe stress. Eliminating the stressors is not easy but there are ways you can do it.

Don't try to control everything

People have the tendency to control everything: their time, money, and other people. What they don't know is that they get most of the stress comes from trying to control everything. It's not bad to be carefree every once in a while. Give yourself some freedom by not thinking about your bills at home, your work deadlines and the traffic jam outside. Recognize that at the moment these things are out of your control.

You can avoid thinking about them. Change your mindset. You can use the analogy of a dresser. In the bottom drawer you can store all your stresses and worries. In the top drawer you can store all your happy thoughts and things you're grateful for. So if you're having difficulty changing your mindset or thoughts, go ahead and place them in the bottom drawer and grab something from the top one.

Spend one hour a day without technology

It is true that technology plays an important role in people's lives. However, it is also true that it takes up a large part of one's time. People are meant for interaction and socialization. Though technology, like smartphones, tablets and computers are meant for communication, people nowadays forget and do not seem to bother talking with their classmates, co-workers and neighbors. It is as if their minds have been taken over by these gadgets.

These gadgets can be a source of additional stress. Spending one hour a day (or longer) without them would be a helpful way of relieving your stress. It can be very challenging for some to not check their email or look at their phone for even one hour. Instead of interacting with your smartphone or computer, talk with the people around you, laugh out loud with them and share stories with them. You'll see how refreshing and energizing this can be.

For more information on strategies for telling stories, and strategies for talking to strangers and making new friends, check out: ***The Storytelling Method***, and ***The Conversation Method***, which will give your social life a new set of wings.

Take a Time Out

Time out is for those who are brave enough to take a step back and rethink of everything. Taking a timeout does not mean giving up; it just means that there are some things that you need to take care of before proceeding to the next step. In a sense, it's a way to unwind and look at the big picture and refocus on what is important about whatever you are currently working on.

Stress often results from too much work and not giving your body or mind enough time to relax. Give yourself a break from working. Taking short work breaks each hour increases productivity. Even a short 2 – 5 minute break to stretch your body, or 5 minutes to walk around or 5 minutes to step outside and get some fresh air will help. When you continue working despite exhaustion, you may produce unsatisfactory results that can further aggravate your stress. Some people like to meditate and others like to take a walk to clear their mind. So go ahead and take that time-out.

Live in the present moment

Most of the anxiety, worry, and stress that you feel arise from thinking about the future or the past. You stress about 'what if's'. What if you did this or what if you did not do that? You worry whether it's going to rain or whether you can meet the deadline of your assignment. Live in the present so that much of your worries and anxiety will be eliminated. A rule I like to use is the 80/20 rule – spending 80% of my time enjoying the present moment, and 20% of my time thinking of the future or what I can learn from my past. Life is most fun and relaxing when you are enjoying the present moment.

If you want to learn more about how to live in the present moment, I highly recommend my book titled ***How To Live In the Present Moment,*** which has proven to be an eye-opening experience for many readers.

Chapter 15

Learning to relax

THE TWO RELAXATION POSITIONS

Lie on the bed on your stomach, with shoulders and neck relaxed, mouth half closed, arms along the hips, palms of hands resting on the mattress, legs outstretched, slightly apart. This is the position in which it is easiest to relax. It is advisable to adopt it until you become proficient in the technique.

Sit in a comfortable armchair, with a high backrest, then rest your head, keeping it relaxed. Place the palms of your hands on the armrests, keep the knees bent, the legs slightly apart and the soles of your feet firmly on the ground. This position can be adopted, with a great advantage, as it can be taken anywhere, when you learn the relaxation technique thoroughly.

EXERCISES

EXERCISE 1

In the chosen position, focus your attention on your right arm, imagining that it is covered with sand: this way you will be able to feel its heaviness. After a few seconds, focus your attention on your left arm, always thinking that it is under the sand, so you will feel its heaviness on this one too. Proceed in this way, passing first to the right leg and then to the left one. In a short time, you will be able to feel the whole body heavy and relaxed. Keep relaxing for a few minutes, repeating the phrase "I feel calm," or imagining that you are surrounded by nature .

EXERCISE 2:

After performing the first exercise, you will feel a slight feeling of cold, because the relaxation causes a slight drop in body temperature (about one degree). At this point with the mind you have to rebalance this phenomenon by saying: "my right arm is warm"; and then again: my left arm is warm," and so also for both legs and concentrating, from time to time, on each of them. Continue until you can feel a pleasant warmth.

EXERCISE 3:

Focus your attention on your breathing, lulled by its cadence and trying to imagine the path that the air takes once it enters your lungs, both during inhalation and exhalation. After entering into mental harmony with your breath, imagine that you are on a sailboat, immersed in the absolute silence of the sea. At this point repeat the sentences: "I am happy and relaxed, nothing in the world can frighten me; I can face anything and win.

Where To Find These Limiting Beliefs

How do you find out what beliefs are blocking you?

A limiting belief always comes in the form of "I can't feel x without y." An example of this is, "I can't feel loved without a partner," or, "I can't feel secure without a job," or, "I can't feel confident while being at a certain weight." Knowing this narrows down the problem beliefs somewhat.

So, do you just read positivity books and go through changing these kinds of beliefs one by one? Do you just keep doing a process of trial and error until you get what you want? And when you find the belief, how do you change it?

If you've been into personal development or the law of attraction for a while, you've probably tried talking yourself out of certain beliefs, only to experience them coming back to haunt you. You might be able to believe a new empowering belief for a time through scripting and affirmations, but eventually the same frustrations in your life rear their head again and again.

The key **is,** you can't change a belief on paper. You have to make change it emotionally**. Why?**

Limiting beliefs are held in place by emotions. Specifically, repressed emotions like fear, sadness, guilt, shame, or anger. We don't generally want to explore or test these beliefs, because of the emotion that is associated with them.

Emotions are like glue to these beliefs. When you find out what the belief is and you try to talk your way out of it, unless you experience an emotional shift (which you will feel), the glue holds that limiting belief in place.

Where does this emotional glue come from?

Emotions want to move. They are a natural flow of feeling that you experience. But, when you believe "I can't feel x without y" you block your own emotional flow.

On top of that, many people have limiting beliefs regarding their emotions themselves. One I had for a long time was, "It's not ok to feel anger." So, whenever I felt angry I would try to repress it. These kinds of beliefs cause you to stuff all of these emotions. When you stuff these emotions, they harden into glue and attach to the beliefs that they hold in place. So, when you try to change your beliefs, you often have to shift the corresponding emotion.

Since those emotions will have been chronically repressed, you'll have to let them out. **Letting them out means feeling them**.

Emotions aren't your enemy

Even though they can feel wretched sometimes, emotions aren't the bad guy. In fact, they are very helpful indicators of the corresponding limiting belief.

So the first beliefs you'll need to change in order to do this work is any regarding feeling those emotions fully in the first place. If you're not comfortable with feeling depression, sadness, shame, guilt, anger, fear, or frustration, then you will have great difficulty changing these beliefs.

It's ok to feel these feelings. You may think that you can't feel them because if you do, you'll always feel that way.

This is how I felt when I was depressed. I was clinically depressed for 10 years of my life. I didn't feel like doing much of anything. I didn't feel passionate about much. I would cry pretty often. I would sleep a lot. But, I was a functional depressive. I had a job. I had friends. They couldn't see what was happening underneath my normal actions, so no one understood what I was going through. I just started thinking that this lack of energy was ok. I started identifying with it. Now that you know more about emotion, can you see how my energy was stuck?

Recently I saw a life coach who asked me what I thought depression was. I replied, "It's fixation on something that doesn't serve me." She said, "No, it's actually repressed emotion, specifically anger." Repressed anger? Wait, didn't I have a belief about that?

So instead of letting the anger out, I manifested depression. I did this in part, because keeping a lid on my emotions is what's considered manly. Men are taught not to identify with their emotions and be as logical and calm as possible at all times. No matter your gender, if you express your emotions fully, you can be seen as emotional which often means unstable. In this way, society pressures us not to stay in touch with our emotions.

Yet, experiencing your emotions fully is exactly what sets you free from your own limiting beliefs and their accompanying emotional glue. When you change your beliefs by letting your emotions out without judgement, you take back the power of your attraction capabilities.

www.ingramcontent.com/pod-product-compliance
Lightning Source LLC
LaVergne TN
LVHW010224070526
838199LV00062B/4715